Original title:
Life's Purpose: To Keep Us on Our Toes

Copyright © 2025 Creative Arts Management OÜ
All rights reserved.

Author: Cassandra Whitaker
ISBN HARDBACK: 978-1-80566-090-3
ISBN PAPERBACK: 978-1-80566-385-0

Balancing Acts Between Doubt and Trust

On a tightrope high, I wobble and sway,
Thinking of breakfast, did I eat today?
The ground looks quite far, but not far enough,
To practice my art as a juggler of stuff.

With my doubts in one hand and trust in the other,
I stumble, I tumble, oh brother, oh brother!
Each step's a new thrill, a comedy show,
Balancing life in this three-ringed tableau.

In the Mosaic of Experiences

Tiles of bright colors that clash and that gleam,
Mixing up laughter with the occasional scream.
Every shard tells a tale, a giggle, a sigh,
In the art gallery of me, oh my, oh my!

Stuck in a corner, I paint with a brush,
Creating confusion, oh what a rush!
A masterpiece grows with each crazy blunder,
In this crazy canvas, I drift like thunder.

The Spiral of Discovery

Round and around, oh what a dizzy ride,
Finding hidden treasures where secrets abide.
Questions like squirrels jump everywhere,
Chasing my tail with a flip of my hair.

In the loop of the spiral, I trip on my feet,
Collecting odd tidbits, oh what a treat!
Each twist is a riddle, each turn is a jest,
In this game of confusion, we're all put to test.

The Dance of Decisions

To boogie or not? Oh, what's the right call?
Twirl left on a whim, then right, oh so small.
The rhythm of choices makes my heart race,
With all of these options, I'm losing my place.

A cha-cha of questions, a tango of fears,
I'm spinning in circles, suppressing my tears.
But give me a wink and I'll step on your toes,
In this dance of decisions, anything goes!

The Heartbeat of Adventure

A squirrel on a quest, oh what a sight,
Chasing dreams and nuts with all its might.
It forgot where it hid, in a fit of glee,
Now it's just zooming like a wild bee.

Each twist and turn, a joyous fall,
With laughter echoing, we heed the call.
Balancing on branches, oh what a thrill,
This squirrel's mischief gives us a chill.

Following the Muse of the Moment

A cat in a hat, prancing so proud,
Struts through the park, drawing a crowd.
It pounces on shadows, oh what a show,
Mistaking a leaf for an elusive foe.

The dog thinks it's play, joining the chase,
But finds himself lost in this odd race.
With every wrong turn and twist of fate,
In the name of fun, they celebrate late.

The Call of the Spontaneous

On a hot summer's day, why sit and stew?
Let's toss off our shoes for a plunge or two!
A picnic's announced, food everywhere,
But a squirrel pilfers, without a care.

Now as chaos reigns, ice cream flies high,
A hasty retreat, but oh me, oh my!
Laughter erupts as we chase the mess,
In the fight for our snacks, I must confess.

Navigating the River of Time

A fish with a wish swims up with a grin,
It dreams to leap high, but keeps splashing in.
As waves of the current pull him askew,
He giggles as he nearly flies right through.

Time's silly dance makes us twirl and sway,
Not a single soul knows just how to play.
But with laughter and joy, we give it a whirl,
And treasure each moment as we do a twirl.

The Whirlwind We Call Existence

In a world that spins and twirls,
We chase after dreams like squirrels.
With twists and turns, we take the leap,
And laugh at the mess we often keep.

Some days we strut, some days we trip,
Like a sailor lost on a rocking ship.
Yet through it all, we grin and jest,
Embracing chaos like a fun-filled quest.

A Compass Lost in the Forest of Choices

In a forest thick with paths galore,
Each step we take just leads to more.
A compass spins like a wild dance,
As we tumble fatefully, given a chance.

Do we go left, or take a right?
Perhaps we'll just follow the light.
With every turn, we laugh and sway,
Enjoying the game in our own zany way.

The Art of Walking Between Shadows

Between the light and dark we stride,
Tiptoeing on the silly side.
With playful jabs and witty sighs,
We juggle fears wrapped in disguise.

Balancing acts on a tightrope line,
With goofy grins, we feel just fine.
For in the shadows, we find our way,
And frolic through the bizarre ballet.

Navigating the Rivers of Resilience

In rivers deep, with currents fast,
We paddle hard, but life's a blast.
With laughter loud and splashes wide,
We steer our boats with zany pride.

Mishaps happen, oh, what a scene!
Like fish on land, we flop and glean.
Yet in each ripple, we learn to cope,
Rowing on waves of never-ending hope.

The Flux of Everyday Miracles

Woke up today, tripped on my shoe,
Coffee made me jitter, oh what to do?
Spilled some on the floor, it's now a brew,
A dance with my mug, who knew it could woo?

The cat looks at me with a mischievous grin,
What chaos will he unleash? Let the games begin!
Chasing feet, zigzag, through thick and thin,
We've turned my tidy home into a circus spin.

Anchored in the Whirlwind

Told myself today, I'd tidy my space,
But the vacuum cleaner joined the race.
It roared and it hummed, left a coat of dust,
Had to bribe it with cookies; fair trade, a must!

Plans went awry, a sandwich on deck,
Sliced off my finger; what a real wreck!
Bandaged in laughter, I'll eat my words,
Sometimes you find joy in the quirkiest herds.

Spinning Threads of Serendipity

On my morning jog, I stumbled, quite spry,
A squirrel dropped his acorn, oh me, oh my!
It rolled into traffic, a natural flair,
The world's a stage—just catching my air!

Friends gathered 'round to hear my tale,
Of squirrels and acorns and a near miss for sale.
We laughed 'til we cried, our bellies did shake,
Life's little hiccups are the best kind of cake.

Navigating Through Winds of Change

Weather's a trickster, they said it was fine,
But my umbrella's in pieces, tangled like twine.
Danced in the puddles, I slipped—what a show!
My reflection just chuckled; 'Where do you go?'

Each gust of the wind brought a new surprise,
A flock of wet pigeons dropping from the skies.
We congregated on streets with laughs on our breath,
Finding joy in the chaos, in nearly all mess.

Flames of Passion in the Mist

In a world where chaos reigns,
We dance amidst the silly pains.
Chasing dreams as they slip by,
With a giggle and a hearty sigh.

Coffee spills and shoes askew,
Yet here we are, a motley crew.
We dash and dive through life's wild race,
Wearing joy like a vibrant lace.

Life's quirks can twist us, that's a fact,
But we'll never be inclined to act.
With humor as our guiding star,
We'll embrace every bizarre spar.

So raise a toast to endless jest,
In this mad dance, we find our best.
With laughter echoing in the mist,
Our worries fade, they don't really exist.

The Glimmer in Everyday Life

Sunrise winks with a cheeky grin,
While birds complain about the din.
Plates are spinning, not just my head,
In this circus, we laugh instead.

A sock's gone rogue, it's on the run,
Chasing the lost dreams, oh what fun!
With mismatched shoes, we strut our stuff,
In the grand game of 'just enough'.

Stuck in traffic, where time stands still,
We crack jokes while looking for thrill.
Finding joy in mundane sights,
Life's a stage with silly lights.

So here's to the chuckles, big and small,
Finding glimmers in the daily sprawl.
In this delightful, awkward strife,
We toast to the beauty of everyday life.

Embracing the Unexpected Journey

Set out with a map that's upside down,
Wanderlust brings us to this town.
Every twist leads to surprise,
In this carnival of the wise.

Lost my way? Just grab a cone,
Adding sprinkles to the unknown.
With laughter, we brush off the blame,
Every misstep ignites the flame.

The road is bumpy, full of quirks,
Running into unexpected jerks.
Yet we dance through all the woes,
With giddy hearts, our journey goes.

So let's embark with zest and zeal,
For life's a ride with a funny wheel.
In this wild trip, we find delight,
Embracing the chaos with sheer delight.

The Fragility of Routine

Morning routines can use a twist,
A cereal box that's gone amiss.
Why not try a dance instead?
With breakfast grooves, we forge ahead.

The clock ticks fast, but we are slow,
Tangled in the day's to-do flow.
Yet when the coffee spills anew,
We laugh it off, it's nothing new.

The sidewalk cracks call out our names,
Stumbling over life's quirky games.
In routine's hold, we bump and sway,
Finding delight in the cliché.

So let's embrace our wobbly fate,
With silly dances, we won't be late.
For in the fragile, there's a cheer,
A reminder that fun is always near.

The Tapestry of Fleeting Moments

Each day unfolds a silly plan,
Like juggling spoons or being a fan.
We chase the dreams that swiftly fade,
In parks where kids play tag with shade.

With laughter echoing through the air,
We trip on our toes, unaware.
In this dance of chaos and cheer,
We find our joy, year after year.

Grains of Sand in the Hourglass

Time slips through like sneaky sand,
We try to catch it, but it's bland.
Like trying to hug a cloud afloat,
Or wearing socks inside a boat.

Each grain whispers, 'What's your next act?'
We juggle choices, that's a fact.
Flip a coin, take a chance,
And let the universe lead the dance.

The Weight of Endless Choices

In a world of options, we scratch our heads,
Should I wear the blue or the red threads?
With candy-coated dreams, we stride,
Collecting whims like jellybeans wide.

The menu's long, it's quite absurd,
Should I speak or say not a word?
In this buffet of funny fate,
We laugh at choices, it's never late.

Teetering on the Edge of Now

We balance on the line of today,
Like kids on swings who want to play.
One foot here, the other there,
In this dance, we breathe the air.

With silly tricks and funny falls,
We navigate through life's odd halls.
And though we wobble, giggles rise,
We rock this life, under bright skies.

Swaying to the Rhythm of Chaos

In the dance of morning coffee,
spills lead the way,
A twist and a turn, oh so frothy,
who needs ballet today?

A dog on a leash, in a tug-of-war,
I'm the one who's swayed,
He chases a squirrel, a mad little chore,
and I'm all dismayed.

The cat naps with regal flair,
while I trip on a shoe,
Oh, the chaos, the sparkling air,
keeps my heart feeling new.

We laugh at the mismatched socks,
life's little prankster show,
In this rhythm, no ticking clocks,
just jump and let it flow!

Whispers of the Unseen Gifts

A note in the fridge that says 'Eat Cake',
the gift of surprise,
Underneath it, a cat's tail, a quake,
oh, such clever spies!

Forgotten keys in the couch so deep,
treasures lie within,
The joy of the hunt, oh the secrets we keep,
where do we even begin?

Unexpected rain on a sunny plan,
but umbrellas don't mind,
We'll dance in the downpour, a whimsical band,
laughing, the joy blind.

So let's toast to the shenanigans grand,
and the joy that it brings,
In life's wacky wonders, hand in hand,
we'll dance and we'll sing!

The Pull of Wanderlust in Still Waters

A goldfish dreams of the ocean's roar,
in its bowl, it feels grand,
Maps of adventure taped by the door,
oh, the wanderlust band!

The chair sings tales of faraway lands,
while socks plot a scheme,
Together they weave fate in their hands,
chasing that curious dream.

A potted plant with a longing gaze,
begging for hiking trails,
With roots secured, it subtly sways,
the heart it avails.

When life gives you calm, throw in some zest,
and sail without fear,
For even a goldfish can plan a quest,
and taste joys that are near!

A Tapestry Woven with Fragile Threads

Each thread a laugh, a tumble, a fall,
sewn into my quilt,
A fabric of chaos, covering all,
with memories built.

From mismatched buttons bright and bold,
to laughter that weaves tight,
We stitch our stories, laughter untold,
like stars in the night.

Grandma's knitting, a clumsy array,
her yarn tangled tight,
Yet, in her smile, she draws us to play,
turning chaos to light.

So here's to the moments, both silly and sweet,
to every odd drape,
In this crazy quilt, our hearts take seat,
oh, life's just a shape!

The Dance of Uncertainty

Twirl and spin, oh what a show,
We dance with doubt, just let it flow.
With every misstep, laughter erupts,
In this grand waltz, surprise disrupts.

A twist, a turn, a step amiss,
Each stumble leads to newfound bliss.
As partners scatter, we leap in joy,
Uncertain rhythms, a child's play toy.

Steps of Serendipity

Trip on a crack, find a dime,
Stumble on fortune, all in good time.
Who knew today would lead us here?
Laughing at fates, we toast with cheer.

A skip, a hop, a joyful mistake,
Each twist of fate, a tasty cake.
Slice of the unexpected, yum, oh yes!
In this clumsy dance, we feel so blessed.

Waking Dreams in the Fretful Dawn

The coffee brews, a sleepy haze,
In bleary-eyed dreams, we wander ways.
A pillow fight with the morning sun,
In this sleepy duel, we laugh and run.

Each snooze button pressed, a naughty tease,
"Just five more minutes!" we say with ease.
But with each yawn, a new day calls,
In waking dreams, we rise and fall.

Balancing on a Tightrope of Time

Step right up to the line so thin,
With a wobble and giggle, let the fun begin.
Time flips and flops, a circus delight,
We juggle our moments, all day and night.

Oh look, here comes an unexpected breeze,
Watch out for laughter, it's bound to tease.
In this high-flying act, we take a chance,
With each little misstep, we join in the dance.

The Mirage of Certainty

In the desert of plans, we stride,
Promises made, our dreams collide.
With a fountain of doubt sprouting near,
We sip on our hopes, but it's mostly air.

We chase after rainbows, ooh and ah,
Only to find just an old shoe and straw.
In the mirage of what we think we see,
We stumble on rocks of uncertainty.

Twists and Turns of the Compass

My GPS recalibrates with glee,
As I drive in circles, oh woe is me!
Left, then right, a zigzag dance,
Who needs a map when you have chance?

A compass that spins like it's gone awry,
Points to adventures, I don't know why.
With each wrong turn, new comical sights,
I find more joys in my whimsical flights.

The Fabric of Improbable Paths

Threads of mishaps woven anew,
Stitching a cloak that fits like a zoo.
With buttons of laughter and pockets of fun,
Each step I take says, 'Look what I've done!'

Patterns of chaos, yet oddly so neat,
In a fabric of fumbles, I find my beat.
Crafting a quilt of what's gone astray,
I warm up to errors that come out to play.

Steps Taken in the Dark

In the cavern of night where I tiptoe around,
I step on squeaky toys; oh, what a sound!
Blindly I wander, a dance of the clumsy,
Tripping on dreams; it's ever so funny!

The path's a surprise with each little move,
I'm grooving to rhythms that never quite prove.
With a misstep here and a giggle there,
In the dark, my purpose brings laughter to share.

Steps in a Winding Path

I tripped on a thought while lost in time,
A shoe string mishap, oh how sublime!
With each tumble down, I learn to rise,
Finding joy in the bumps, what a surprise!

Each step a giggle, each turn a jest,
Who knew missteps could lead to the best?
I dance with the awkward, the stumble divine,
A laugh and a grin, and all will be fine!

The path twists and twirls like a twisty straw,
I'm dizzy from trying to follow the law,
Of walking straight, but hey, why not sway?
The winding fuzz has a part to play!

So raise your glasses to the silly strolls,
Where falling's just part of the hilarious roles,
For on this path, let laughter compose,
A whimsical journey, where whimsy flows!

Embracing the Unknown

I peek around corners with curious glee,
What chaos awaits? Is it friend or is he?
A whispering breeze or a black cat's meow,
In the land of the strange, I make my vow!

So here's to the weird and the wacky unknown,
I'll dance with the shadows, I'll never feel lone!
Each mystery tickles my toes and my brain,
Embracing the funny, with no ounce of pain!

I summon my courage, and jump in the fray,
Chasing wild creatures that lead me astray,
A dragon? A llama? Who knows what I'll see?
The unknown's a party, just wait for me!

With laughter my compass, I wander and roam,
Every twist makes the bizarre feel like home,
To embrace what's offbeat takes bravery, yes,
But oh what a ride, in this comedic mess!

When Shadows Whisper Dreams

The shadows have secrets that tickle my toes,
They dance in the twilight, wearing funny clothes.
As they whisper sweet nothings, I can't help but grin,
For what is a dream, but a giggle within?

They beckon me closer, with flickering lights,
Twisting and turning in whimsical flights,
A parade of oddities, lurking in night,
With laughter as lanterns, I embrace the fright!

Each shadow's a character in a comedy play,
Chasing my thoughts as they dance and sway,
So I join in the rumble, in the soft moonglow,
Where dreams tumble out, and the laughter will flow!

In the murmur of darkness, where silliness dwells,
The shadows spin tales as they jingle like bells,
In the whimsy of whispers, we frolic untamed,
For every sweet chuckle can't stay unexplained!

Chasing Curved Horizons

I saw a horizon that curved like a smile,
Inviting me closer, just stay for a while!
With each step I take, it giggles away,
Making me run in a curious ballet!

The horizons play tricks, oh what a tease,
They dance with the clouds, they frolic the breeze!
I chase them like dreams, they shimmer and shift,
With a bounce in my step, they're the ultimate gift!

Mountains and valleys in a wiggly spree,
Like a party balloon that just can't sit free,
Oh, what a spectacle, colorful, bright,
Chasing the giggles, I'll dance through the night!

So here's to the chase, with a wink and a nod,
For those curved horizons that leave us all awed,
With laughter our guide, and joy as our goal,
We'll follow the whimsy that tickles the soul!

Breathing Life into the Uncertain

Waking up with socks that don't match,
Coffee spills, what a glorious catch.
The cat thinks it's the king of the hall,
As I dodge his furry, spontaneous brawl.

Juggling dreams while dodging old socks,
Praising my skills when my phone finally talks.
Work emails ping, yet I stare at my bread,
Life's quirks become the best guide instead.

I step on a toy and almost take flight,
Who knew that a Lego could give such a fright?
Yet in the chaos, I find something neat,
A strange little rhythm, a whimsical beat.

Some days are lemons, some days are pies,
With each silly mishap, I learn how to rise.
Through stumbling and fumbling, I grow and I laugh,
Breathing life into chaos—my chosen path.

The Echo of Future's Embrace.

Skipping in puddles beneath cloudy skies,
Glimpsing the future through mud-splattered eyes.
Time feels like pudding, so thick and so sweet,
Yet here I am, dancing on clown shoes with feet.

Dogs chase their tails, as I chase a thought,
The grill's on fire, despite what I sought.
Plans made in Lego blocks tumble and fall,
But hey, isn't that the best part of it all?

Futons become boats in a sea of old socks,
While I wear my pajamas as a fashion paradox.
Future's calling me with a wiggly grin,
I trip on my dreams but still manage to spin.

With laughter in hand and a joke on my lips,
Each bump in the road earns a few silly quips.
So here's to the echoes, both near and afar,
Guiding us onward like a sneaky little star.

The Dance of Uncertainty

Waltzing through life on spaghetti-like feet,
Twirling around woes as I juggle and cheat.
Each step is a riddle wrapped in a pun,
Oh look! A banana peel—let the dancing begin!

Uncertain days float like balloons in the sky,
Spinning in circles, then—oh, why, oh why?
I tango with doubts while the laundry's on spin,
And slip on a sock that my dog thought was kin.

Fearing the future? Just do the cha-cha!
Bring your best moves and don't worry, ha-ha!
The music might falter, but who needs a cue?
Let's shimmy through life, just a silly hullabaloo!

Mistakes can be fun, like confetti in spring,
So grab your partner, it's your turn to swing.
With laughter as tempo, we'll dance through it all,
Embracing the stumble, we rise when we fall.

The Quest for Balance

Tightrope walking with a broomstick in hand,
Some days I fly, but don't quite understand.
Eggs in one basket, or just on my plate?
Balance is tricky, but isn't it great?

Juggling work, snacks, and an endless to-do,
One task gets done, but four more break through.
Like a juggling clown at a circus so bold,
Laughing at mayhem, I rise from the fold.

Coffee in one hand while I balance the rest,
And who needs a tutu when pajama pants vest?
I stumble and giggle, it keeps life alive,
The quest for sweet balance, helping me thrive.

So let's tiptoe lightly in this clumsy charade,
Turning each misstep into a grand parade.
In the balance of chaos, we find our cool flow,
The quest leads us onward, with each silly toe.

The Lighthouse of Guiding Stars

In the foggy night a beacon beams,
Shining bright, or so it seems.
But dolphins dance and seagulls squawk,
While sailors trip and fish just walk.

Amidst the waves, we might just miss,
A seaweed salad, oh what bliss!
Tales of barnacles, wisdom's ploy,
Who knew they teach a buoy to toy?

A lighthouse keeper with hat so tall,
Shouts at fish — they heed his call.
Yet the starlit path is a slippery ride,
With flippers and fins now acting as guides.

As boats sway under moonlit beams,
Who knew they'd take up ballet dreams?
For in this jest of cosmic spree,
We stumble, giggle, and just be free.

Tracing Routes Against the Tide

Maps all tattered, adventures await,
With a compass that thinks it knows fate.
But here I stand, feet in the sand,
As the ocean laughs at my grand plan.

Loop-de-loops, what a silly path,
Every wrong turn sparks a hearty laugh.
Fish wave hello as they swim by,
While I chase crabs, oh me, oh my!

Seagulls squawk, they plot our fall,
With every wing flap, they con us all.
Yet in the mess, wisdom we find,
To let the tide lead — oh, what's the grind?

So let's embrace this winding quest,
For chasing dreams is the ultimate jest.
With nature's humor as our guide,
We ride the waves, come splash or slide!

While the World Keeps Turning

Spinning tops and dizzy flares,
Jumping jacks in office chairs.
The clock ticks on with silly grace,
As I stumble through this funny race.

Coffee spills and muffins fly,
As deadlines pass, we laugh and sigh.
With every twist the world presents,
We juggle chaos — what's the suspense?

Calls dropped, with a flustered grin,
Missed the point, but did we win?
For in this dance of frantic hurt,
We mix our drinks, and life's dessert.

Wheels of fortune spin away,
With jokes and puns, we seize the day.
So let them turn, while we take flight,
In this whirling giggle of pure delight!

Flickers of Inspiration

With a spark of light, ideas ignite,
In the kitchen chaos, what a sight!
Pasta flops and sauce takes flight,
Dinner's a mess, but oh, delight!

Ideas fly like popcorn zest,
We chase them down, a comic quest.
Should we paint or sing a song?
Wait, was that the dog all along?

Doodles dance across the page,
Who knew chaos could be all the rage?
As brushes sweep and colors blend,
We find our joy — each twist, a friend.

So here's to whims that brightly glow,
Inspiration's flicker steals the show.
Let laughter fill this crazy ride,
For in the mess, our dreams collide!

Echoes of What Could Be

A penguin dons a tux, quite dapper and neat,
He slides on ice with a flair that can't be beat.
Yet when it comes to fish, he struggles all day,
Just paddling in circles, what a clumsy ballet!

The cactus dreams of oceans, imagining waves,
While the fish yearns for sun, pretending he braves.
But who could have guessed, in this puzzling play,
That life's just a circus, no clear game to play?

A tiger paints stripes on a traffic cone,
Wonders if 'really' he's trying alone.
A turtle moves fast, as fast as he dares,
While the hare's sipping drinks, tossing back golden flares!

As birds write their songs in the morning sun's light,
Each note hints at journeys that might just take flight.
Yet gravity chuckles, keeps us on the ground,
With echoes of dreams in a laughter profound.

The Tension of Tomorrow's News

A cat in a hat jumps up on the news,
Meows about fancy, predicting odd views.
But who can decipher when mischief's afoot,
That leaves all the cats in a perplexed trot?

The goldfish watches, behind glass he schemes,
While a dog in a tux rehashes old dreams.
In a world full of headlines that twist and that shout,
The truth seems to sneak in, a curious bout!

A squirrel on a quest for the perfect acorn,
Finds his stash raided, oh what a scorn!
He glances at headlines that make him feel taxed,
While the hedgehog just chuckles, all cozy and relaxed.

The issues are tangled, like yarn in a pile,
Each twist leads to laughter, with plenty of style.
For every bold headline that raises some fuss,
Tomorrow's just waiting to gather the dust.

Chasing Horizons with Outspread Wings

An owl wears sunglasses, looking quite cool,
Swooping low and singing, not adhering to rules.
As squirrels with helmets zoom past on their bikes,
Chasing the sunset, like adventurous hikes!

A stork in the distance complains of the heat,
While flamingos gossip, tumbling to their feet.
With toes in the sand, they stretch and they play,
Embracing the madness, chase worries away!

The seagull spots fries, takes a casual dive,
In search of the thrill, they feel so alive.
As world spins around them, a dizzying ride,
With laughter and chaos, they take it all in stride.

On the edge of the universe, dreaming of fun,
They dance in the sunlight, from dusk until dawn.
For every horizon, a jest makes it bright,
And joy fuels the chase 'til the stars spark the night.

The Flicker of A Candle's Doubt

A candle flickers, trembling in the breeze,
As shadows gather, plotting mischievous tease.
But the moth, with its dance, buzzes 'round with delight,
In a tango of fate, they sway in the night.

The candle wonders if it's too soft to stay,
While the matches conspire to light up the play.
They giggle in fables of warmth and some wax,
As flames whirl and swirl, they'd play sneaky tracks!

Bees buzz in circles, not caring a bit,
While a pyromaniac tries to make a lit skit.
But the smoke gives a wink, brings laughter and cheer,
As the flamethrower cabbage shouts, "No worries, my dear!"

In a world full of flames, the tease carries on,
With giggles and grins that happily dawn.
For in flickers of light that dance with some doubt,
The charades of existence keep us giggling out loud!

The Pivot of Possibilities

In a world of choices vast and wide,
We dance around like we've got no pride.
Should we take the leap or just stand still?
Maybe a donut? Yes, that's the thrill!

With options fluttering like butterflies,
We stumble forward, often in disguise.
A jogger's grace? Oh, what a tease!
I trip on thoughts while I aim to please.

Juggling dreams like a clown on parade,
Trip over wishes, but never dismayed.
Witty detours full of charm and fun,
Let's laugh together, we're never done!

So here's to the pivots we didn't foresee,
Turning left when we meant to flee.
With every misstep and every cheer,
We dance through life with a wink and a jeer.

To Leap or to Linger

To leap or to linger, now there's a thought,
One foot in the air, don't forget what you've sought.
Maybe I'll jump or perhaps I'll just watch,
My lazy old cat, yeah, she makes the bestotch.

With each curious moment that pops up anew,
I ponder the path or the couch, what to do?
Do I dive into chaos or stick with my tea?
The thrill of a leap—oh, what's it to be?

A leap of a fried egg from the morning pan,
A lingering glance at the Oompa Loompa clan.
Maybe just wait for the bus that won't come,
Laughing and chuckling while others just run.

So, leap like a frog or stay like a snail,
Follow your whimsy, you won't ever fail.
In this dance of the awkward, I giggle and grin,
For every day's chance, let the mischief begin!

When the Road Twists Unexpectedly

I thought I was headed straight to the mall,
But who knew a twist could lead to a stall?
A fork in the road, and where to begin?
Oh, hello there, squirrel! Let the games begin.

The GPS says go but it changes its mind,
"Re-routing," it chirps, how could it be blind?
A left turn to tacos, a right turn to fries,
Every turn brings a giggle, what a surprise!

Yet here comes a detour, a sign all amiss,
I stumble through laughter, who'd want to be this?
With rollercoaster paths and a few happy shrieks,
I revel in chaos, it's fabulous peeks.

Shall I steer through the potholes and puddles of life?
We chuckle and swerve through all sorts of strife.
Let the road twist and turn, oh what a show,
We'll dance on this journey, wherever we go!

The Joy of the Unwritten

In a script yet to pen, oh what will we say?
The thrill's in the pauses, not just in the play.
With empty pages, we frolic and flirt,
Creating our moments, unseen and overt.

What nonsense awaits in a future unknown?
Each blank line's a chance to take it full grown.
Do I scribble a joke or a wild twist of fate?
With a sprinkle of humor, oh, isn't that great?

Here's to mischief masked in scribbles and doodles,
Our hearts go on wild, like a herd of poodles.
Each unexpected laugh, a diamond that shines,
Binding our stories in playful designs.

So, let's celebrate pages that wait to unfold,
With giggles and wiggles, this life is pure gold.
The joy of what's coming, no reason to fret,
We'll pen it together—let's not take the bet!

The Symphony of Balance

In the circus of daily strife,
Clowns juggle dreams, oh what a life!
Horns honk softly, a dog steals a shoe,
As we tiptoe through chaos, yes, me and you.

Laughter and chaos, a marvelous blend,
On this tightrope, we twist and we bend.
With every misstep, we dance and we sway,
Who knew balance could be such a play?

The juggling act never quite ends,
With each little slip, our humor transcends.
A pie in the face, oh, what a surprise,
In this symphony, no need for rehearsed ties.

So let's dance and giggle, make no mistake,
It's the joy in this mess that we truly make.
In the rhythm of wobbles, we find our groove,
Embracing the wild, we laugh and we move.

Dancing in the Rain of Possibilities

Umbrellas pop out like mushrooms in spring,
While raindrops delight and the birds start to sing.
Puddles reflect all the dreams we hold tight,
As we twirl in the droplets, hearts light as a kite.

Slippery sidewalks? A chance to embrace,
A spontaneous tango, oh what a race!
With each little splash, we leap in delight,
Dancing in weather, it feels just right.

Glistening streets in their silver attire,
Who needs a sun when the clouds conspire?
We'll shimmy and shake, let the world see,
That dancing in rain brings pure glee and glee.

So grab your galoshes, let's boogie right here,
In the puddles of life, there's nothing to fear.
With every misstep, we just laugh and spin,
For life's vibrant dance is about the fun within.

Signs on the Road Less Traveled

A fork in the road, oh what shall we choose?
One says to potluck, the other to snooze.
With signs that are silly and arrows askew,
We'll follow our whims like a bird that just flew.

Detours and laughter, a map made for fun,
Who needs a GPS when joy's just begun?
With every wrong turn, we find hidden gems,
Like a llama in slippers or a car full of hems.

Roadblocks may etch frowns on design,
Yet each bump and hiccup's a part of the line.
So let's hoot like owls when we swerve and we veer,
As unexpected adventures draw ever so near.

With snacks packed in to share on the go,
And laughter that echoes, our spirits will glow.
Every detour a story that needs to be told,
On this merry road trip, let's embrace being bold.

The Surge of Unexpected Waves

Surfers ride life on a board full of thrills,
With every new wave comes laughter and spills.
From wiping out hard to popping back up,
The ocean of chance fills our very own cup.

Splashing and crashing, the sea's quite a muse,
For every wild wave is just ours to choose.
With no perfect form on this bumpy sea,
We stumble and giggle, just you and me.

Seashells are treasures, and driftwood's a friend,
As we ride each swell, we can surely depend.
That life is a beach, unpredictable too,
Just hold on tight, and dance with the blue!

So pack up your worries and dive into play,
In the surge of the moment, we'll find our own way.
With board shorts a-flapping and spirits all high,
We'll ride the wave of joy, let's spread and fly!

The Pulse of a Moving Heart

A jellybean in my shoe, oh no,
It's rolling like a lost balloon.
With every step, it bounces high,
I trip and laugh, but still, I try.

Chasing dreams like a squirrel on caffeine,
Dancing through life, silly and keen.
The heartbeat quickens, the feet keep pace,
In this crazy race, I find my place.

With each stumble, a lesson learned,
Like burnt toast, but still, I'm turned.
Every misstep a step towards glee,
Who knew life's dance was waltzing me?

So here I am, a clown in tow,
With laughter as my guiding glow.
The pulse of a heart that skips and hops,
Embracing mishaps, never stops.

Navigating the Maze of Existence

A map in hand, but none to see,
I'm lost in thought, where could I be?
Round and round in circles I go,
It's like playing tag with a shadow.

Got cheese for brains, they whisper wise,
Yet often I forget, and that's no surprise.
But bumpy paths make the best of tales,
Each twist and turn, where laughter sails.

Zigzagging life's quirky quest,
With breadcrumbs left at every fest.
A signpost reads, 'Turn left, go right,'
I grin and choose to dance in delight.

Navigating this joyous maze,
With a goofy grin, in a playful daze.
And when I find the cheese at night,
I'll cheese it up with all my might!

Beyond Comfort's Embrace

Snuggled tight in my cozy chair,
The world outside? Who would dare?
But comfort's web can sometimes sting,
Like a surprise visit from a bee's zing.

They say, "Step out, grab life by the horns!"
But outside lurk both laughs and scorns.
A brave soul with rubber ducky dreams,
Finds courage in the silliest schemes.

A trampoline of messy plans,
Bouncing high while laughter spans.
Comfort's lure may hold me still,
But wild adventures give me a thrill.

So I leap beyond, arms open wide,
Flipping, flopping, on this wild ride.
Beyond the couch, where the giggles race,
Life's a circus—let's find our place!

When Stillness Speaks

In silence, whispers gently tease,
Like a cat who purrs, but with great ease.
When stillness speaks, it's a funny chat,
It's the moment I forget where I sat.

A stroll through quiet, with jumbled thoughts,
Like searching for gold in a shoebox of knots.
Each pause a joke, wrapped in delight,
Weaving tales beneath the moonlight.

The world at rest can play a tune,
A funny little hum beneath the moon.
I might just chuckle at shadows I see,
For stillness holds a circus in me!

Beneath the calm is a thriving scene,
Where giggles bubble and dance unseen.
So here's to the quiet, the calm, the mirth,
With stillness as my goofy hearth!

The Jigsaw of a Restless Heart

In pieces scattered on the floor,
A puzzle that we can't ignore.
With corners missing, shapes askew,
We laugh at what we thought we knew.

Each twist and turn, a silly chase,
Finding out we're out of place.
With every try, our hopes revive,
Perhaps the chaos helps us thrive.

Our hearts might race, or take their time,
In any rhythm, we can rhyme.
The jigsaw fits, it seems, just so,
As life skews left, we twist and go.

So grab a piece and take a seat,
Let's mix it up, and feel the beat.
Who knew the heart could be this fun?
Now let's just dance until we're undone.

Moments that Defy Definition

A wink at fate, a glimmer bright,
We fumble through, but what a sight!
A purple cat with polka dots,
We stumble while we take our shots.

Tickling time, with mindless stares,
Defining moments like thin air.
With every laugh, we build a frame,
To capture joy, or is it lame?

Beneath the chaos, giggles sprout,
In simple sights, we twist about.
What's real or not can be a blur,
But who needs sense? Let's just confer!

So dance with those who know the lines,
And giggle hard at tangled signs.
Moments that twist and turn with ease,
Are just like breeze, with endless tease.

Beneath the Surface of Everyday

Underneath the mundane hum,
A wacky world can make us dumb.
With socks that don't quite find their pairs,
We surf on dreams with crazy flares.

The coffee spills in morning light,
Frustration turns into delight.
A bird with sneakers takes a flight,
While we laugh at our silly plight.

Beneath the noise, there's laughter's spark,
In silly things, we make our mark.
With every fumble, every jest,
We find in chaos, we're truly blessed.

So join the joys that life bestows,
Embrace the silly, that's how it goes.
In madness sweet, our hearts will bloom,
And find the fun amidst the gloom.

Guarding the Essence of What Is

A squirrel in shades watches the scene,
While we chase ducks that might be mean.
In everyday quirks, we find the gold,
And guard the tales that need to be told.

Bouncing through the park, we play,
Telling jokes that lead us astray.
With every giggle, we hold the charm,
Protecting laughter from any harm.

Through ups and downs, we dance around,
Holding tight to joy we've found.
An essence rare that fills the air,
In funny moments, we learn to care.

So let's embrace each twist and turn,
With every laugh, there's more to learn.
Guarding the fun, we wear a grin,
As life throws curveballs, let's dive in!

Hurdles in the Journey

I tried to walk a straight line,
But tripped over a shoe, oh so fine.
Dancing with the curb, what a show,
Each step's a tumble, go with the flow.

A fence I swung over, like a pro,
But landed in a patch of pesto.
Life throws lemons? I'm making a pie,
The path's a circus, oh my, oh my!

With every stumble, a chuckle or two,
Chasing butterflies, with socks that are blue.
The hurdles are funny, not scary at all,
Just laugh it off when you trip and fall.

In this mad, merry race, no need to fret,
Adventures await, and regrets? Forget!
Leap over the chaos, let out a cheer,
For every mishap, brings joy quite near.

The Rhythm of Unforeseen Changes

I woke up to a sunny surprise,
But the clouds were sneaky, oh those guys!
Dancing with raindrops, my hair went wild,
Each step ahead felt just like a child.

Life plays a tune, a fiddle or drum,
I tap my feet, then my phone goes numb.
The playlist shuffles, oh what a laugh,
I'm jigging with traffic, stuck in half.

But when the rhythm feels way offbeat,
I twirl and spin, make it feel sweet.
All the detours are a shallot's delight,
In this waltz of changes, my laugh takes flight.

The dance floor is life, with quirks and flair,
With every misstep, I soar in the air.
So here's to the crazy, the twists and bends,
Unforeseen changes, oh how it transcends!

Breathing to the Beat of Tomorrow

I woke up panting with shoes on the floor,
What a way to start, who needs to explore?
I breathe in the chaos, exhale a grin,
Tomorrow's a dance, so let's dive in!

Every new day brings quirky delight,
With cereal flying, I'm ready for flight.
The clock tick-tocks, and I race with flair,
Breathing the moments like fresh mountain air.

Laughter erupts like a bubbly fizzy drink,
I bounce on the couch, then I trip on the sink.
Waltzing with chaos, take one step at a time,
Every tumble's a giggle, like silly old rhyme.

So here's to the mornings, zany and bright,
Chasing tomorrow with all of my might.
Each breath a reminder, come what may,
Life's a party, come swing and sway!

The Spark in the Unpredictable

One day it's sunny, the next it's a freeze,
Life's full of sparks that will tickle and tease.
I wear mismatched socks, a crown on my head,
Unpredictable days, where laughter's widespread.

A squirrel steals my snack, it runs with such glee,
I chase it in circles, oh, what a sight to see!
The winds whirl me round like a wild twirl,
Every moment's unexpected, a shimmering pearl.

Tickling the chaos with bubbles and cheer,
Dancing through puddles that suddenly appear.
Life's a surprise filled with joy and delight,
A spark in the chaos, igniting the night.

So bring on the twists, the turns, and the rides,
With giggles and snorts, let's conquer the tides.
For in the unpredictable, I find my true self,
Just grab a few sparkles, let's dance on the shelf!

Footprints on the Path of Wonder

In sneakers bright, we race ahead,
With maps of dreams—who needs a bed?
Each step a dance on paths unknown,
   Tripping over hopes we've sown.

The world's a stage, or so they say,
  But tripping's part of the ballet!
With laughter loud, we leap and twirl,
Chasing the winks of this wild whirl.

Sometimes we stumble, fall, and roll,
Like marbles lost, we chase the goals.
  A funny slip, a wobbly glide,
The best of plans we just can't hide.

With every footprint left behind,
We find the fun that's intertwined.
So grab your shoes and off we go,
To wacky places we can't outgrow.

When the Ground Shifted Beneath Us

Oh dear, the ground just pulled a prank,
With cracks and quirks, we walked the plank.
We balance on this wobbling floor,
Searching for laughs and much, much more.

The earth winks up, a trickster bold,
Turns our steps into tales retold.
With giggles shared and arms out wide,
We'll hold on tight, let's enjoy the ride!

The shifts and shakes, oh what a sight,
We dance through chaos, feel the light.
If the ground won't stop its funny jig,
We'll join the game—oh man, this gig!

So when the earth starts acting strange,
Let's wobble and giggle, rearrange.
Together we'll laugh with all our might,
And chase the moments, pure delight.

Embracing the Unfamiliar

New paths unfolding, what's this place?
With quirks and turns, we join the race.
In lands unknown, we find a spark,
Where every corner hides a lark.

With strange cuisine and funky sights,
We dance with joy on unusual nights.
A little fear, a lot of cheer,
Who thought adventure brought such beer?

Let's hug the weird, make friends with weirdos,
In rollercoasters of life's endless phases.
The unexpected's like pop rocks in soda,
A burst of fun, oh what a quota!

So here's to strange, we welcome you,
With open arms, we'll try what's new.
Together we'll shimmy, wiggle, and sway,
In the dance of life, we'll find our play.

The Tune of Unwritten Journeys

With each step forward, songs arise,
A melody of chuckles and surprise.
The unknown rhythm, our hearts compose,
On paper maps, we scribble prose.

With laughter soaring, we spin around,
In this grand orchestra of the ground.
Play the note that feels so right,
Let the journey spark delight!

The paths unwritten call us near,
With joyful beats, we dance in cheer.
A silly tune, a heartfelt choir,
In every stumble, we find our fire.

So strum the strings of endless days,
In the dance of life, we find our ways.
Our unwritten journeys, a giggle-smart,
Shall keep us moving, hand on heart.

The Wanderer's Dilemma

A map with no directions, oh what a sight,
I wandered in circles, from morning to night.
With every wrong turn, I stumbled and fell,
My shoes now look like they've danced through a hell.

The coffee line grew until I lost track,
Counting each cup, I should head on back.
But the barista's grin is a joy to behold,
So I'll stay just a bit, for the stories they've told.

I asked for advice, and a squirrel replied,
"Just keep moving forward, enjoy the ride!"
Its nutty philosophy, quite hard to refute,
Perhaps a wild chase is what I should pursue.

But as luck would have it, I tripped on a log,
A dodge from a car that looked like a frog.
I laughed at my folly, tossed my worries aside,
Turns out the journey's the best kind of ride!

In the Labyrinth of Lifetimes

In a maze full of mirrors, I'm lost for good,
Thought I'd come to get snacks, but I'm misunderstood.
Each turn I take echoes with giggles and sighs,
Why are there so many places to hide from the pies?

With bread rolls and crumbs piled high to the sky,
I dance like a fool as the pastries all fly.
A pie in my face, oh it's a classic mistake,
But laughing's my specialty, make no mistake!

The walls whisper secrets, quite mad in their tone,
"Follow the laughter, you're never alone."
So I twirl and I spin, just enjoying the ride,
In the labyrinth of lifetimes, I take it in stride.

But the cheese vendor's lurking, oh what a mess,
"Just a bit of gouda can lighten your stress!"
With a smile and a wink, he sends me away,
To chase my next snack in this comical play!

Horizons Beyond the Horizon

Standing on cliffs, I squint at the sea,
With wild dreams soaring, just like a bee.
But wait, is that ocean? It's just a mirage,
I'm staring at puddles in my own garage!

My friend said to travel, to take to the sky,
But all I can find is a robot nearby.
He dances like crazy, with a beep and a blip,
A seaside adventure right here in my trip!

I built my own jetpack with forks and some glue,
Ready for altitude, it's just a grand view.
But all it does currently is give me a fright,
As I wobble and stumble and hope for the flight!

Yet laughter erupts with each silly mistake,
Maybe horizons are made for the take.
The journey's the treasure, my map's just absurd,
Why not laugh at my dreams, haven't you heard?

Unfolding the Map of Dreams

With a crumpled old map that's marked with some stains,
I search for delight through the puddles and drains.
Each landmark is quirky, a rollercoaster ride,
With a sign saying: "This way to joyous pride!"

I stepped on the gas(pump) at the corner store,
But the snacks yelled, "No! There's so much in store!"
Between chips and a chocolate, I danced with glee,
Who knew my true treasure was just a spree?

The map led me here, to this tumbleweed's fate,
Where dreams tangle up in a comical state.
I laughed 'til I snorted, in my life's little play,
What mattered most was the fun in the fray.

So I'll crumple this map, smile wide from the heart,
In the wild of the world, I've mastered the art.
To lead with a giggle, that's the secret it seems,
Every twist and each turn just unfolds more dreams!

The Art of Staying Afloat

In the pool of dreams, we splash and dive,
Dodging all the ducks, just trying to survive.
We float on noodles, laugh at gravity,
Wobbling on our whims, that's our strategy.

Mismatched socks and shoes on the wrong feet,
We dance through life with two left beats.
A latte spill, a trip on the curb,
Yet every mishap, we give a curve.

Like a cat on roller skates, we sway,
Balancing hopes in a quirky way.
With quirks and giggles, we'll twist and twirl,
Navigating chaos like a waltzing girl.

So here's to the dance, the jumbled spree,
Embracing blunders, wild and free.
With each silly slip, we learn and grow,
In the art of afloat, we steal the show.

Echoes of Spirited Motion

With a spring in our step and mischief in mind,
We chase down the snacks, no moment left behind.
A banana peel here, a pie in the face,
In this wacky race, we've found our place.

We tiptoe on sidewalks, avoiding the cracks,
As if dodging monsters lurking in packs.
Our purpose is laughter, to prank and to tease,
Turning each fumble into a breeze.

Like a squirrel on caffeine, dashing about,
Life's an arcade, and we're all about.
With each little stumble, we leap even higher,
In the spirited motion, we never tire.

So let us embrace all the silly mistakes,
And dance through the chaos that life often makes.
With giggles and gaffes, we'll waltz through the fray,
In the echo of motion, we'll shout, "Hip-hip-hooray!"

In the Thicket of Ambition

In a jungle of dreams, we swing like apes,
Climbing up branches, avoiding the tapes.
With a grin on our face and mud on our shoes,
We navigate the thicket, finding our cues.

A plan here and there, like a game of charades,
With ideas that sprout like the wildest cascades.
We trip over roots but giggle, not pout,
Each fall's just a chance to learn more about.

Dodging the thorny tasks we avoid,
Through twists and turns, our joy is employed.
With dreams as our compass and whimsy as guide,
In this bush of ambition, let's take a slide.

So here's to the mess and the scramble of dreams,
In the thicket of life, nothing's as it seems.
With laughter our armor, we'll boldly proceed,
In the game of existence, we'll follow our lead.

Skating on the Edge of Reality

With a twist and a turn, we glide on thin air,
Balancing life like a skater's flair.
The edge of absurdity's beckoning call,
We leap with a laugh, won't stumble or fall.

In the rink of our thoughts, we spin and we slide,
Chasing the mirage of a rollercoaster ride.
With popcorn in hand and a friend at our side,
We whirl through the madness with flair and with pride.

When the world gets wobbly, we add a new spin,
With giggles and chuckles, we dive right in.
The secret to balance? Just let go of tight,
Skating through blunders with joy and delight.

So let's twirl through the chaos, in sparkles and glee,
On this edge of bizarre, we dance wild and free.
With laughter as fuel, we'll continue our quest,
Skating through life, we've turned it to jest.

Juggling Dreams and Delays

With dreams stacked high like Jenga blocks,
I dance and twirl around the clocks.
Another task? I drop a few,
Laughing as I chase the brew.

Procrastination's a jolly game,
My to-do list looks quite the same.
I juggle life with silly flair,
Who needs structure? Not a care!

The Canvas of Spontaneity

Painting my day with happy mess,
Throwing colors, why not guess?
A brushstroke here, a splash of fun,
Oh look, it's a cat on the run!

Each moment's brush is bold and bright,
I waltz through chaos, what a sight!
Creating art with every blunder,
Life is a show, full of wonder!

Rising with Every Mistake

I trip and fall with a goofy laugh,
Each tumble's just a new autograph.
With every goof, my spirit sings,
I've mastered the art of flapping wings!

Like toast that lands on buttered side,
Mistakes are where I take great pride.
I bounce right back, a rubber ball,
Life's hiccups? They just enthrall!

In the Footsteps of Fate

I dance on paths both strange and winding,
Lost my way, oh, how I'm finding!
Fate's footprints lead me here and there,
In mismatched shoes, I do declare!

I twirl around the twists and turns,
In every slip, a lesson learns.
Chasing fate with a clumsy grin,
Adventures start where you begin!

Paths Interwoven in Time

We dance upon this winding road,
With mismatched socks, a heavy load.
Each turn we take, a strange parade,
Of socks and shoes in a wild charade.

Laughter echoes in every bend,
Like silly clowns that will not end.
With every step, we trip and tease,
Finding joy in moments that please.

The sun may shine; the rain may pour,
Yet here we are, always wanting more.
With twirls and tumbles, we will prance,
Embracing awkwardness in our dance.

So let's confound the straightest line,
With wobbly paths, oh how they shine!
In this chaos, there's a subtle rhyme,
A melody played in the dust of time.

The Joys of the Bumpy Ride

Roller coasters, ups and downs,
We throw our hands like kings and crowns.
The joys of life can make us squeal,
With every bump, we can't conceal.

A pit stop here, an error there,
With tangled hair and laughing stare.
We juggle tasks, a hurried dance,
While sipping tea from our own pants.

In wobbly cars, we swerve and slide,
Chasing dreams we cannot hide.
With squeaky wheels and tunes off-key,
We find our bliss, oh can't you see?

So hold on tight, dear friend of mine,
For this wild ride is quite divine.
Embrace the bumps, the joy, the thrill,
And laugh it off, you've got the skill!

The Threads of Chance and Fate

Life's a tapestry, bright and wild,
Each thread a chance, a curious child.
Some knots are tight, while others fray,
We weave our stories, come what may.

A slip of thread, a playful chase,
With frizzy curls, we find our place.
Stitch by stitch, we change the game,
With mismatched patches, we're never the same.

So gather 'round, let's sew our glee,
With silly patterns for all to see.
In every twist, in every turn,
New tales are waiting; we all shall learn.

For in this quilt of chance and fate,
We find our rhythm, it's never late.
So grab a needle, let's make it fun,
In this crazy craft, we're all as one.

In the Realm of Unfinished Stories

Once I tried to bake a pie,
But it ended up a total lie.
The crust was hard, the filling sweet,
I dropped it twice, what a defeat!

I scribbled thoughts on paper fine,
But half the letters danced in line.
I tell my friends it's art, you see,
They nod and smile; they pity me!

Plans I make just fall apart,
Like jigsaw pieces with no heart.
But isn't chaos somewhat fun?
I've mastered games without a gun!

So here's to tales left in the dark,
A laugh, a joke, a tiny spark.
In this realm of not quite done,
I find my joy, I'm still the one!

The Spark in the Overcast Sky

Clouds above, a heavy load,
Yet here I dance upon the road.
With gum on shoe and hair in air,
I laugh and spin without a care!

The drizzle falls, I glide and slip,
Each foible's just another quip.
I shout to friends, "Join in the rain!"
We'll make a mess, embrace the pain!

Umbrellas flip, like boats we sail,
Through puddles deep, we laugh, we wail.
The spark inside just won't be still,
It lights the gloom and gives a thrill!

So take your frowns and toss them high,
Let silliness reach for the sky.
In overcast, we find our light,
With laughter shared, the world feels bright!

Caught Between Dreams and Reality

Woke up late, my head in dreams,
Socks don't match, or so it seems.
Coffee spills like life's own game,
I grin, I laugh, I take the blame!

Thoughts of work dance in my head,
But all I want is my soft bed.
A spreadsheet waits, a nightmare's cue,
Oh, will this day end too soon too?

I juggle whims, like colorful balls,
My plans take flight, then promptly fall.
Yet in this chaos, I find glee,
Between the dreams, I find the me!

With every stumble, every trip,
I learn to laugh, not let it rip.
Embrace the mess, the odd and weird,
For in this dance, I've truly steered!

The Call to Unraveled Adventures

Adventure calls, oh where to go?
The couch looks nice, but I say no!
I'll pack a bag, with snacks in tow,
Set out to think where did the time go?

Maps are fun, but GPS is sly,
It reroutes me, oh my, oh my!
A wrong turn leads to secret spots,
Where petty fights turn into rots!

Unraveled twists upon my quest,
I meet new friends, it's all the best.
We share our tales over ice cream,
Reality fades; it's like a dream!

So here's to journeys, weird and wide,
Through laughter, mishaps, and crazy rides.
The call to roam sparks joy anew,
In the chaos, I find my true crew!

www.ingramcontent.com/pod-product-compliance
Lightning Source LLC
Chambersburg PA
CBHW051643160426
43209CB00004B/775